The Kitchen Witch

Infusing Magic into Cooking and Nourishment

The Kitchen Witch: Infusing Magic into Cooking and
Nourishment

Contents

An Introduction to Kitchen Witchery 4

Setting Your Magical Space: The Kitchen 10

The Alchemy of Ingredients 16

Intuitive Cooking and Magical Manifestations 22

The Magic of Herbs and Spices 27

Moon Magic and Lunar Infused Cooking 33

The Power of Teas, Tinctures, and Elixirs 38

Magical Baking and Sweet Spells: The Enchantment of the Oven 43

The Witch's Garden 50

Seasonal Witchery and Sabbat Feasts 55

Nourishing Body and Spirit: Mindful Eating 61

Rituals and Blessings for the Kitchen Witch 67

The Magic of Fermentation and Preservation 72

Sacred Smoke: Incense and Smudging in the Kitchen 77

The Kitchen Witch's Book of Shadows 83

Kitchen Witch Meditations 89

Embracing the Path of the Kitchen Witch 95

An Introduction to Kitchen Witchery

Imagine this: a warm kitchen, fragrant with the scent of roasting vegetables and baking bread, filled with the soft light of a setting sun seeping in through the window. There is a pot of soup simmering on the stove, stirred by a woman who pours her heart and soul into the creation of nourishment. Every stir is a blessing, every spice added a spell, and the kitchen, her sacred space. This picture is a vivid portrayal of a Kitchen Witch in action.

Kitchen witchery, at its core, is the act of transforming ordinary tasks of cooking and cleaning into magical rituals. It is about creating and nourishing, about understanding the profound relationship between the food we eat and the life we live. In essence, it's about infusing magic into the mundane.

Origins and Evolution

The roots of kitchen witchery are ancient and far-reaching, connecting to practices found in different cultures across the globe. It's tied to the tradition of the hearth and home being the epicenter of family and community life. Our ancestors had a deep understanding of the land, seasons, and cycles of nature, and they recognized that preparing food wasn't just a mundane task, but a magical one.

These beliefs were passed down through generations and morphed into what we now know as kitchen witchery. It's a flexible, eclectic practice that doesn't adhere to a rigid set of rules or belong to a particular culture or religion. Instead, it's a collection of practices that honor the sacredness of the home and hearth, combining elements of folk magic, green witchcraft, and elements of modern Wicca.

Basic Principles of Kitchen Witchery

The essence of kitchen witchery lies in its fundamental principles, which revolve around intentionality, mindfulness, and connection to the natural world.

Intentionality: A kitchen witch infuses everything they do with purpose and intention. Each ingredient is chosen for a reason, every action imbued with meaning. The intention may be to create a meal that will help heal illness, foster love, or provide protection.

Mindfulness: Being a kitchen witch requires mindfulness. It's about savoring each step, from selecting ingredients to the chopping, stirring, and finally serving the meal. It's about being present in each moment, recognizing the magic inherent in these everyday actions.

Connection to the Natural World: Kitchen witchery also requires a deep connection with the earth and the cycles of nature. It involves understanding the magical properties of herbs, plants, and other ingredients. It also means respecting and honoring these elements, striving for a sustainable approach in the kitchen.

Infusing Magic into Everyday Rituals

At the heart of kitchen witchery is the belief that magic exists in the everyday, in the ordinary. It's in the meals we prepare for ourselves and our loved ones, in the cup of tea brewed with care, in the bread baked with joy. This magic, however, doesn't manifest itself. It requires the witch to acknowledge and cultivate it consciously.

The magic in kitchen witchery is about energy and intention. It's about realizing that when you cook, you're not just combining ingredients. You're blending energies. For example, a rosemary-infused dish is not just flavorful; it's also protective due to rosemary's protective properties.

As a kitchen witch, your tools aren't just your cauldron and wand but your pots and pans. The spells you cast are your recipes, each ingredient carefully chosen for its magical correspondence. And your Book of Shadows? It might well be a recipe book filled with generations' worth of family meals and secrets, annotated with notes about the magical properties of different ingredients.

Moreover, a kitchen witch sees the act of cooking as a ritual, turning the preparation and consumption of food into a sacred act. This could be as simple as taking a moment to express gratitude for the food before eating or as complex as performing a full-fledged ritual, complete with casting a circle and calling the quarters, before beginning to cook.

Nourishment as a Spiritual Act

Finally, kitchen witchery recognizes that nourishment goes beyond the physical. Yes, we eat to fuel our bodies, but we also eat to feed our souls. The food we eat can affect our energies, influence our emotions, and connect us to the earth and the cycles of life and death.

As a kitchen witch, preparing food becomes a spiritual act, a way of showing love and care for oneself and others. It becomes a form of healing magic, where a bowl of soup can comfort a sorrowful heart, and a slice of homemade bread can ground us in the present moment.

Kitchen witchery isn't just about cooking. It's a way of living, a path that recognizes the sacred in the everyday and the magical in the mundane.

It's a path that transforms the act of nourishment into a form of communion – with ourselves, with others, and with the universe. And it all begins in the heart of the home – the kitchen.

Setting Your Magical Space: The Kitchen

In the world of kitchen witchery, the kitchen is far more than a place to prepare meals. It is a sanctuary, a workshop, and a magical playground where everyday ingredients are transformed into nourishing food that not only feeds the body but also the soul. Setting your magical space within the kitchen forms the backbone of your craft and journey as a kitchen witch. Here, we will explore how you can create a kitchen brimming with positive energies, select the right tools, and make it an ideal place for practicing kitchen witchery.

Part I: The Kitchen - Your Sacred Space

Just as an artist finds inspiration within the confines of their studio, the kitchen is where a kitchen witch finds their own creative muse. It's a space to create, to experiment, and most importantly, to infuse magic into every dish.

Start by examining your current kitchen space. Is it warm and inviting? Does it inspire creativity and the desire to nourish? Does it have a clean, free-flowing energy, or does it feel cluttered and stagnant?

Remember, kitchen witchery isn't about having a grand, perfectly decorated kitchen. It's about creating a space that is conducive to magical work, a space that feels alive with energy, and a space that feels like your own. A small kitchen with a few simple utensils can be just as magical as a large, well-equipped one, if it's filled with love and good energy.

Begin by decluttering your kitchen, as an organized kitchen helps maintain the flow of positive energy. Remove any items that aren't essential to your cooking or your craft. These can disrupt energy flow and make your space feel congested and chaotic. Once you've decluttered, maintain cleanliness and order. As the saying goes, "cleanliness is next to godliness," and in the case of kitchen witchery, this couldn't be more true.

Part II: Choosing Your Tools

Every witch needs her tools, and the kitchen witch is no exception. These tools act as conduits for your intentions and energies. They are your allies in the magical work that you do in the kitchen, so choosing them wisely is crucial.

Your basic kitchen witch tools include the cauldron (a cooking pot can play this part), a knife (an athame), a wooden spoon (a wand), a mortar and pestle (for grinding herbs and spices), a broom (or besom, for energy clearing), a chalice (for holding liquids), and a pentacle (a plate or cutting board can be this).

Select your tools with care. They should feel right in your hands and bring you joy when you use them. You can add other items over time, such as crystal bowls, cast-iron skillets, or a particular set of measuring cups that appeal to you, but remember, it's not the tool itself that holds the magic, but your relationship to it.

Part III: Energizing Your Space

Once your kitchen is decluttered and your tools selected, the next step is to charge the space with positive energy. There are various ways to do this.

First, you can cleanse the space. This can be done by smudging using herbs like sage, rosemary, or lavender, or by sound using bells or singing bowls.

Next, invite positive energy into the space. Place crystals that resonate with the energy of kitchen witchery, such as carnelian for creativity, rose quartz for love, or clear quartz for amplifying intentions, in strategic spots in your kitchen.

A simple kitchen altar can serve as the heart of your kitchen. This could be a corner of your counter or a shelf where you place items that inspire you or represent your magical intentions. You could include a favorite cookbook, a plant, a candle, or a bowl of fresh fruit. Change the items on your altar with the seasons to keep the energy fresh and relevant.

Lastly, consider using color to boost the energy of your kitchen. Different colors hold different energies and can be used strategically to enhance your space. For instance, red can inspire passion and energy, blue can bring calm and healing, green can inspire growth and abundance, and yellow can invoke happiness and creativity.

Part IV: Your Personal Energy

Your personal energy is an essential ingredient in your magical kitchen. Make sure to approach your kitchen work in a good mood, with a clear mind and an open heart. Negative energy can seep into your cooking and affect not just the taste of your food but the magic you're attempting to weave.

If you find yourself in a negative state of mind, take a few minutes to meditate or perform a grounding exercise before you start cooking. Remember, cooking is an act of love, and it's this love that helps turn the ordinary into the magical.

Creating a magical kitchen space is a unique and personal process. The key is to remember that your kitchen is a reflection of you and your craft. So, whether you're stirring a pot of soup or baking a loaf of bread, remember that you're not just cooking, you're creating magic.

By setting your magical space, choosing your tools with intention, and ensuring your kitchen brims with positive energy, you create a haven where you can enjoy the craft of kitchen witchery.

A place where every slice, simmer, and stir holds the potential to be a magical act. A place where food is not just prepared, but also celebrated as a beautiful and magical gift of the earth.

The Alchemy of Ingredients

The heart of kitchen witchery lies in the ingredients we use. The vegetables and fruits, herbs and spices, grains and nuts, all have unique properties, both physical and metaphysical, which influence not just the taste, color, and texture of our dishes, but also their energy vibrations. Every ingredient in our pantry is potential magic waiting to be tapped into. But to utilize this magic to its fullest, we must understand its nature. This chapter delves into the spiritual properties of various food items, herbs, and spices, and their role in influencing our wellbeing and spiritual growth.

Understanding the Spirit of Ingredients

Every ingredient has a spirit, an essence, which is a potent combination of its flavor, aroma, color, shape, and texture. This essence often mirrors the ingredient's magical properties. Consider an apple. Its round shape and the hidden star when it's cut in half is often associated with magic, mystery, and the divine feminine. Its sweet, crisp taste symbolizes abundance and happiness. This understanding of the ingredient's essence forms the basis of ingredient alchemy.

Elemental Associations of Ingredients

Just as the Universe is made up of five elements – Earth, Water, Fire, Air, and Ether (Spirit) – so too are our ingredients. Each ingredient aligns with one or more of these elements and can influence our energy accordingly. Root vegetables like carrots and potatoes are aligned with the Earth element, symbolizing grounding and stability. Ingredients like seaweed and fish, being water-dwelling, resonate with the Water element, symbolizing emotions and intuition. Spices like chili and ginger, with their fiery kick, are aligned with the Fire element, signifying transformation and action. Ingredients such as lemons and apples, which grow high on trees, resonate with the Air element, symbolizing intellect and communication. The Spirit element, or Ether, is a bit different. It is more about how the ingredients are used, their purpose, and intent, rather than a specific list of ingredients.

Magical Properties of Common Ingredients

Now that we understand the fundamental principles of ingredient alchemy, let's explore the magical properties of some common kitchen ingredients:

Salt: One of the most commonly used ingredients, salt, is a powerful cleanser and purifier. In kitchen witchery, it's often used in recipes for protection, banishing negativity, and promoting health.

Garlic: Garlic is renowned for its protective properties. It's a staple in dishes that aim to repel negative energies or when you're seeking strength and courage.

Cinnamon: Cinnamon is linked with fire and sun energy, making it perfect for spells or recipes intending to draw success, prosperity, and passion.

Basil: Associated with love and wealth, basil can be used in recipes to attract both. Its bright, uplifting flavor corresponds with joy and happiness.

Ginger: Ginger's spicy kick is a reflection of its magical properties. It's used to ignite passion, enhance spiritual growth, and draw in success and power.

Apple: As already discussed, the apple's magical associations are with knowledge, wisdom, and the divine feminine. Use apples in dishes when seeking enlightenment or spiritual growth.

Rosemary: Known for its properties of protection and purification, rosemary also aids memory and can be used in recipes when you seek mental clarity or want to make unforgettable meals!

Honey: Honey symbolizes abundance and sweetening outcomes. It can be used when you want to attract love, happiness, or to sweeten the disposition of people around you.

Carrots: With their vibrant color and association with the earth element, carrots are known to improve eyesight both physically and metaphysically, enhancing clarity and wisdom.

Herbs and Their Magical Properties

Herbs have long been revered for their healing properties, but they also hold potent magic. Some commonly used herbs and their associations are:

Thyme: Thyme is associated with courage and bravery. It's also believed to attract loyalty and affection.

Mint: Mint is excellent for spells related to travel or financial success. It's also helpful in invoking good spirits during ritual work.

Sage: Sage is perhaps one of the most famous herbs for its powerful cleansing and healing properties. It's often used in smudging rituals to purify spaces and people.

Parsley: Associated with love, protection, and purification, parsley is often used in purification baths and love spells.

Lavender: Known for its calming and peaceful properties, lavender is used in spells to encourage relaxation, peace, and restful sleep.

Combining Ingredients for Spiritual Growth

The real magic happens when you start combining these ingredients. Understanding the properties of each ingredient allows you to create dishes that not only satisfy your physical hunger but also fulfill your spiritual needs. For instance, a simple dish of pasta with a sauce made from garlic, basil, and tomatoes (for love and passion), seasoned with salt (for purification) and chili flakes (for courage and transformation), can be a powerful love spell. Similarly, a dessert made with apples (for wisdom) and honey (for sweetness and abundance), spiced with cinnamon (for success), can be a tool for manifesting success in an upcoming endeavor.

The alchemy of ingredients is a vast and deeply personal subject. Each kitchen witch may develop their own associations and meanings based on their personal experiences, culture, and intuition. This is simply a starting point. The true magic comes from developing a deep connection with your ingredients, understanding their energies, and creating food that nourishes not only the body but also the soul.

Intuitive Cooking and Magical Manifestations

Intuitive cooking is an approach that elevates the culinary process from being a simple routine to a nurturing, magical experience. As kitchen witches, it's an integral part of our craft to connect with our ingredients, to understand their energy, and to weave that energy into our meals with intention and intuition. This magical interaction forms a bond between us and the food we prepare, creating meals that not only satiate our hunger but also feed our souls and manifest our desires.

The art of intuitive cooking starts with understanding our ingredients. Each ingredient we use, from grains to vegetables, herbs to spices, fruits to nuts, carries its own unique energy. These energies interact with our bodies and spirits, influencing our thoughts, emotions, and physical health. By developing a keen understanding of these energies, we can become more attuned to the needs of our bodies and souls, leading to more balanced and fulfilling meals.

Consider, for example, a simple carrot. On a physical level, it provides essential nutrients, like vitamin A and dietary fiber. However, on an energetic level, the carrot, which grows below ground and reaches deep into the earth, symbolizes grounding and stability. By eating a carrot, you can draw on its grounding energy to bring yourself back into balance and foster a sense of calm and steadiness.

Intuitive cooking is not about following recipes to the letter, but about trusting your instincts and creativity. It's about learning to listen to your intuition when you're selecting your ingredients, deciding how to prepare them, and determining how to combine them. It's about sensing what your body and spirit need at that moment and allowing those needs to guide your cooking process.

When cooking intuitively, you might find yourself drawn to certain ingredients or cooking methods without understanding why. Trust these instincts. They are your subconscious communicating with you, revealing what you need to balance your energy, restore your health, or bolster your emotional well-being.

Remember, intuitive cooking is not an exact science. It's an art, an exploration, an act of self-expression and self-care. It's okay to make mistakes. In fact, mistakes are an essential part of the learning process. Each "mistake" is an opportunity to understand your intuition better, to fine-tune your inner guidance system, and to grow as a kitchen witch.

Now, how do we infuse magic into our meals and manifest our intentions? The answer is simple: through intention-setting and energy manipulation.

When we talk about intention-setting, we're referring to the process of defining what you want to achieve with your meal. Your intention could be anything from enhancing your physical health, to fostering self-love, to attracting abundance or protection. As you cook, hold this intention in your mind, visualize it, and put your energy into it. This practice charges your food with your intention, turning it into a magical meal.

Energy manipulation, on the other hand, involves working with the energies of your ingredients and your tools. It's about understanding the different energy frequencies, how they interact, and how to align them with your intentions.

For example, let's say your intention is to create a meal that encourages peace and tranquility. You might choose ingredients known for their calming energies, like chamomile or lavender. As you prepare your meal, you might stir your pot in a clockwise motion, which in many magical traditions is associated with attracting or "drawing in" the desired qualities. As you stir, visualize peace and tranquility infusing your meal.

This practice becomes even more potent when you incorporate ritual into your cooking process. Simple rituals like lighting a candle, saying a prayer or blessing, or playing calming music while you cook can amplify the magical energy in your kitchen and your meal.

The key to successful magical manifestation in intuitive cooking lies in the belief that the food you prepare is more than just sustenance. It's a manifestation of your love, your care, and your magical intentions. Every bite carries your energy and your desires, radiating them out into the universe.

In essence, intuitive cooking and magical manifestation transform the act of preparing and eating meals into a deeply spiritual experience. It's a form of everyday magic that feeds not just the body, but also the soul. It's a way to practice mindfulness, to connect with the earth and its bounty, and to manifest our desires in a delicious and nourishing way.

As you embark on your journey of intuitive cooking, remember that there's no right or wrong way to do it. It's a personal and individual journey, one that evolves with you and your unique energy. Listen to your intuition, trust in your magical abilities, and above all, enjoy the process. The kitchen is your sanctuary, the ingredients are your magical tools, and the food you create is your spell – a delicious, nourishing spell that manifests your intentions and brings magic into your everyday life.

The Magic of Herbs and Spices

In the realm of kitchen witchery, herbs and spices are more than just flavor-enhancing ingredients; they are potent tools for magic and healing. Each herb and spice carries a distinct vibration, resonating with specific physical, emotional, and spiritual needs. As we journey through this chapter, we will explore the enchanting world of herbs and spices, their magical properties, and how we can harness their energies in our daily cooking rituals.

To begin, let's define what we mean by "magic" in this context. The magic referred to in kitchen witchery is not the spectacle of stage illusions or movie sorcery, but the subtle art of tapping into the underlying energies and vibrations of the universe. When we speak of an herb or spice having a particular magical property, we are referring to its ability to facilitate our intentions and desires, such as promoting healing, attracting prosperity, or fostering love.

Now, with that clarified, let's delve into the world of magical herbs and spices.

Basil: The Herb of Love and Prosperity

Basil, with its vibrant green leaves and peppery scent, is not only a staple in Mediterranean cuisine but also a potent magical herb. It's associated with love and prosperity. Use it in your dishes when you want to foster harmony and affection within your home or when you're seeking financial stability and growth. A simple basil pesto can serve as a powerful tool for infusing your meals with these energies.

Rosemary: The Herb of Protection and Memory

Rosemary, known for its heady aroma and woody taste, is a versatile culinary herb and magical ingredient. It's been linked with protection and memory throughout history. Use rosemary in your cooking when you wish to create a protective barrier around your home or when you need to enhance your memory and concentration. A comforting bowl of rosemary-infused soup can warm the body and spirit, wrapping you in a protective energy blanket.

Cinnamon: The Spice of Passion and Success

Cinnamon, with its sweet, warming aroma and flavor, is a beloved spice in both sweet and savory dishes. In the magical realm, it's associated with heating up passion and attracting success. Sprinkle cinnamon into dishes when you wish to enhance sensuality or draw success into your endeavors. A mug of cinnamon-spiced hot chocolate can not only tantalize your taste buds but also work as a delicious charm for success and passion.

Sage: The Herb of Wisdom and Purification

Sage, a silver-green herb with a pungent flavor, has long been associated with wisdom and purification. It's used in smudging rituals to cleanse spaces of negative energies. You can incorporate sage into your recipes when you seek wisdom or wish to purify your mind and spirit. Sage-infused stuffing or a sage butter sauce not only adds depth to your dishes but also introduces a purifying, wisdom-enhancing element to your meals.

Ginger: The Spice of Power and Vitality

Ginger, a root spice known for its spicy flavor and therapeutic properties, is linked with personal power and vitality. Use ginger in your meals when you need a boost of confidence, strength, or when you're recovering from an illness. A revitalizing ginger tea can serve as a potent brew to infuse your day with strength and vitality.

Thyme: The Herb of Courage and Healing

Thyme, with its tiny leaves and potent flavor, is a magical herb associated with courage and healing. Use thyme in your cooking when you're seeking the courage to face challenges or when healing is needed. A heartwarming thyme-roasted chicken can provide nourishment to the body while imbuing your spirit with courage and healing energies.

Black Pepper: The Spice of Protection and Cleansing

Black pepper, a staple spice found in most kitchens, has protective and cleansing properties in kitchen witchery. Use it to drive away negative energies or cleanse your space of lingering negativity. Peppercorn-crusted steak or a simple peppered soup can serve as a tool for protection and purification.

While this is not an exhaustive list of herbs and spices, these examples provide a starting point for your journey into the magic of herbs and spices. Remember, the key to successful kitchen witchery lies not just in knowing the magical properties of your ingredients but also in preparing and serving them with intention and mindfulness. As you chop, sauté, stir, and simmer, visualize your goals, infuse your intentions, and let your cooking be a tangible expression of your magic.

As a kitchen witch, your culinary creations are more than just meals; they are potent spells, brewed in the cauldron of your kitchen and crafted with the magic of your heart. So, open your spice cabinet, reach for those vibrant jars of herbs, and let the magic unfold in your kitchen.

In the next chapters, we will delve deeper into how you can create magical meals according to the moon's phases, brew magical teas and elixirs, and explore the enchanting world of magical baking. For now, let your senses be your guide as you explore the magic of herbs and spices, and embrace the joy of cooking with intention, reverence, and love.

Moon Magic and Lunar Infused Cooking

Cooking by the moon's phases might sound like an ancient and forgotten practice, yet it is a harmonious, rhythmic cycle that provides us with the opportunity to draw energy from the celestial body closest to our Earth. The moon, with its compelling cycles of waxing and waning, exerts a powerful pull on our lives. In this chapter, we'll explore how to harness these lunar energies into your kitchen, infusing your cooking and nourishment practices with the moon's powerful rhythms.

Understanding the Moon's Cycles

The moon's cycle begins with the new moon, where it appears almost invisible in the night sky, symbolizing new beginnings and fresh starts. As the moon begins to wax, it slowly grows, reaching the first quarter, where it's half visible – a time for taking action and building momentum. As it continues to wax, it becomes the full moon, a time of culmination, celebration, and gratitude. From there, it begins to wane, decreasing in visibility until it reaches the last quarter – a time for reflection and release. The moon then disappears completely, beginning the cycle anew.

New Moon: A Time for Intention Setting and Nourishment

The new moon, with its air of beginnings and opportunities, is the perfect time to set intentions for the coming lunar month. It's a time for soulful, nourishing meals that reflect your aspirations.

A simple ritual for the new moon could involve cooking a meal from scratch, infusing it with your intentions for the coming cycle. This could be a stew, a soup, or a casserole – anything that involves combining ingredients and allowing them to meld together over time.

Try a lentil soup infused with herbs like basil and sage, both known for their properties of protection and prosperity. As you chop your vegetables, stir your pot, and season your dish, visualize your intentions for the coming month infusing into the food. When you consume your meal, envision it providing the nourishment and energy you need to manifest these intentions.

Waxing Moon: The Growth Phase and Cultivating Energy

As the moon grows, so too should your actions and efforts towards your goals. The waxing phase of the moon is a time of increase, growth, and attraction. Now is the time to cook foods that require rising, such as bread or other baked goods.

In this phase, try making a classic bread from scratch. As you knead the dough, infuse it with your desires and intentions. Let it rise under the growing moonlight, symbolizing the 'rising' or 'growing' of your goals. The process of baking, a transformative experience for your dough, parallels the transformation you seek in your life. Enjoy your bread warm, allowing the comforting taste to affirm that your intentions are manifesting.

Full Moon: A Time for Gratitude and Celebration

The full moon is a time to acknowledge growth and express gratitude. It's a time for indulgent, celebratory food - dishes that make you feel abundant and joyful.

In this phase, consider a dessert like a warm apple pie spiced with cinnamon for prosperity and nutmeg for luck. As you prepare your pie, take time to acknowledge the journey you've made since the new moon. When you enjoy your dessert, savor the sweetness as a symbol of the sweet victories and progress in your life.

Waning Moon: Release and Reflection

The waning moon phase is a time for release, letting go, and introspection. It's a time to prepare lighter meals, symbolizing the shedding of any unnecessary burdens or obstacles.

Consider a simple, cleansing vegetable broth infused with herbs like rosemary for protection and purification. As you prepare your broth, meditate on what you'd like to release or let go of. When you consume your broth, envision it cleansing and releasing these energies from your body and spirit.

Cooking with the Lunar Energy

The moon exerts a powerful influence on the Earth and our lives. By aligning your cooking and eating habits with the lunar cycle, you invite a beautiful, rhythmic flow into your kitchen – one that nourishes not just your body, but your soul. Each ingredient, each dish prepared and savored under the changing moonlight, becomes a magical act of alignment with the natural world and the celestial rhythms.

Incorporating moon magic in your cooking also infuses everyday life with intention and mindfulness. Each meal becomes a ritual, a celebration of life's cycles mirrored in the celestial dance of the moon.

As we conclude this chapter, remember that lunar-infused cooking is more than just a practice. It's a dance with the divine, a nod to our ancestors who lived by the moon's glow, and a celebration of the magic that exists within our kitchens, within our pots and pans, and within ourselves. May your kitchen always be filled with the bewitching charm of the moon's magic, and your dishes always nourish body, mind, and soul.

The Power of Teas, Tinctures, and Elixirs

In the world of the kitchen witch, magic isn't confined to spells and rituals; it's intricately woven into the very fabric of our nourishment. As such, the art of brewing teas, creating tinctures, and concocting elixirs holds a special place in our magical arsenal. These potent potions, brimming with the healing properties of herbs and spices, can bring about profound transformation, provide protection, and help in manifestation of our intentions. In this chapter, we will delve into the secrets of these magical mixtures and discover how they can be prepared and used to enhance our spiritual and physical well-being.

The Magic of Tea

Tea, the humble infusion of leaves and water, holds a magic all its own. It is a ritualistic potion, the brewing of which has been perfected across cultures and centuries. Its simplicity belies its power. The right blend of herbs, combined with a specific intention and consumed mindfully, can work wonders. A relaxing chamomile tea before bed can soothe the spirit, a strong cup of rosemary tea can heighten concentration, while a mug of peppermint tea can facilitate clearer communication.

Choosing your tea involves tuning into your current needs. Are you seeking comfort, balance, healing, or clarity? Your intuition will guide you to the right herbs. When preparing your tea, pay attention to the temperature and steeping time. These factors can influence not just the taste, but also the effectiveness of your brew.

While your tea is steeping, close your eyes and visualize your intention. Picture it infusing the water along with the herbs. Feel the magic seeping into the liquid. As you sip your tea, imagine this magical energy being absorbed by your body, achieving the desired effect. This practice turns the simple act of drinking tea into a sacred ritual of self-care and magic.

The Potency of Tinctures

Unlike teas, tinctures are highly concentrated, and their preparation involves the infusion of herbs in alcohol or vinegar over an extended period. Tinctures allow us to harness the medicinal properties of plants in a potent form that can be easily consumed or used topically. While teas offer immediate soothing effects, tinctures work gradually, making them suitable for addressing long-term health and wellness goals.

Creating a tincture begins with selecting a suitable plant material. The chosen herbs are then steeped in a solvent—usually a high-proof alcohol—for several weeks. This extracts the active compounds, after which the plant matter is strained out, leaving a potent tincture. It is important to remember that tinctures can be quite powerful, and therefore should be used in moderation and under the guidance of a knowledgeable practitioner or herbalist.

Like tea, the creation of a tincture can be a magical ritual. As you combine your ingredients, hold a clear intention in your mind. This intention will be infused into your tincture alongside the plant essence, lending it a powerful vibrational energy that aligns with your magical goals.

Energizing Elixirs

Elixirs, on the other hand, are a fusion of the concepts of teas and tinctures, often incorporating sweet elements like honey or glycerine. They can be consumed for their health benefits, as well as for their magical properties. Elixirs are typically used in spell work, during rituals, or when a strong dose of energy is needed.

Creating an elixir is similar to making a tincture, but often includes the step of sweetening and sometimes heating the mixture. As you create your elixir, concentrate on the transformative power of the fire element as it helps meld the ingredients and intentions together.

The Role of Teas, Tinctures, and Elixirs in Healing, Manifestation, and Protection

The magic of these potions lies not just in their ingredients, but in the intention imbued during their preparation. A healing tea might incorporate herbs known for their restorative properties, like echinacea or ginger, but it is the intention of wellness that truly imbues the brew with healing power.

Manifestation elixirs can be crafted to attract love, prosperity, or success. By combining corresponding herbs, and focusing on your intention as you brew and consume your elixir, you align your energy with your desired outcome, attracting it towards you.

Protection tinctures can work in a similar way. Herbs like rosemary, sage, or fennel have long been associated with protection in various traditions. Infusing these into a tincture and consuming it or applying it to your body can serve as a potent protective spell.

Whether you're reaching for the comfort of a warm tea, the potency of a tincture, or the transformative energy of an elixir, remember that it is your connection to the earth, your intention, and your belief in the magic within you and the world around you that truly gives these potions their power. Happy brewing!

Magical Baking and Sweet Spells: The Enchantment of the Oven

There's an old saying that goes, "Cooking is an art, but baking is a science." While this might be true in the mundane world, in the realm of kitchen witchery, baking takes on a magic all its own. Baking, with its precise measurements and specific methods, aligns perfectly with the careful precision often found in spellcasting. Through the process of transforming raw ingredients into mouth-watering sweet treats, kitchen witches can consciously weave intention and magic into every step. In this chapter, we'll delve into the enchanting world of magical baking, exploring how to create pastries, cookies, cakes, and other desserts that are as powerfully charged with magic as they are irresistible to your taste buds.

The Basics of Magical Baking

Baking is alchemy — the art of transmutation. We start with simple ingredients like flour, sugar, eggs, and butter, and through the magical processes of mixing and heat, we transform them into something extraordinary. When we infuse this process with specific intentions and mindful focus, our creations take on the power to manifest love, prosperity, happiness, and more.

The Intention

Like any other magical working, the foundation of magical baking lies in your intention. What are you hoping to manifest? Whether it's love, joy, peace, or protection, have a clear idea of your intention before you begin.

Choosing Your Ingredients

Each ingredient used in baking carries its own magical properties. For example, sugar is traditionally associated with love and attraction, while cinnamon can be used to speed up the manifestation of spells. When choosing your ingredients, select those that align with your magical intention.

Charging Your Ingredients

Before you begin, take the time to charge your ingredients with your intent. You can do this by simply holding each ingredient in your hand, visualizing your intent, and infusing the ingredient with that energy. You can also whisper your intentions or desires into each ingredient or speak them out loud.

The Baking Process

As you mix your ingredients and prepare your dough or batter, continue to focus on your intention. Visualize it manifesting in real life as you stir, and imagine your energy being incorporated into your creation.

When you put your dessert into the oven, imagine the heat acting as the catalyst that brings your spell to fruition. As the ingredients come together and transform into your baked goods, so too does your magic become infused into the treat and begins to manifest in the physical world.

Recipes for Love, Prosperity, and Happiness

In the world of magical baking, every dessert holds the power to manifest different intentions. Let's explore some sweet spells you can bake right at home.

Recipe for Love: Heartfelt Honey Cakes

Honey, an ingredient associated with love and attraction, is the star in this recipe. These delightful cakes can be made to share with a loved one or to attract more love into your life.

Ingredients:

2 cups of flour (for sustenance and grounding)

1/2 cup of sugar (for love and attraction)

1/2 cup of honey (for love and sweetness)

2 eggs (for fertility and abundance)

1/2 cup of milk (for nurturing and motherly love)

A pinch of salt (for protection and grounding)

Charge each ingredient with your intention of love, mix them following your favorite honey cake recipe, and bake with the visualization of love enveloping your life.

Recipe for Prosperity: Cinnamon Sugar Prosperity Cookies

Cinnamon is a well-known prosperity-attracting ingredient. Paired with sugar, these cookies are a potent spell for drawing in abundance.

Ingredients:

2 3/4 cups of flour (for sustenance and grounding)

1 teaspoon of baking soda (for transformation)

1/2 teaspoon of baking powder (for amplification)

1 cup of butter (for richness and dairy blessing)

1 1/2 cups of white sugar (for attraction)

1 egg (for potential)

2 teaspoons of vanilla extract (for added sweetness in life)

1/2 teaspoon of salt (for protection)

2 tablespoons of ground cinnamon (for prosperity and speed in manifestation)

Proceed by charging your ingredients, preparing the dough, and baking them into cookies. As they bake, visualize your home filled with abundance and prosperity.

Recipe for Happiness: Joyful Lemon Bars

Lemons, with their bright color and zesty flavor, are often associated with happiness, purification, and rejuvenation. These lemon bars are designed to bring joy and happiness into your life.

Ingredients:

2 cups of flour (for sustenance)

1/2 cup of powdered sugar (for joy and attraction)

1 cup of butter (for richness and dairy blessing)

4 eggs (for fertility and abundance)

1 1/2 cups of white sugar (for happiness and attraction)

1/3 cup of lemon juice (for joy and happiness)

1/2 teaspoon of baking powder (for amplification)

1/4 teaspoon of salt (for protection)

Follow your preferred lemon bar recipe, and as you prepare and bake, visualize your life being filled with joy, laughter, and happiness.

Sharing Your Sweet Spells

Once your magical treats are ready, it's important to share them with conscious intent. If you've baked a cake for love, share it with your partner, or if you're trying to attract love, offer it to friends and let the universe see your act of giving.

Remember, the magic in your baked goods isn't just about the ingredients or the baking process; it's about sharing your intentions, your joy, and your magic with others. In the end, the most important ingredient in any form of kitchen witchery is love. When you bake with love and share your creations with others, you are casting a powerful spell that resonates far beyond the walls of your kitchen.

The Witch's Garden

Just as the kitchen is the heart of the home, the garden is the soul. For a Kitchen Witch, the garden holds more than just beauty and bounty; it is a place of magic, a source of power, and a vessel of spiritual wisdom. It's where the seeds of your intentions bloom into reality, bringing forth the essential ingredients that find their way into your magical cooking and nourishment rituals.

Creating your witch's garden involves much more than just selecting plants and sowing seeds. It's about understanding the mystical properties of each plant and learning to grow them in harmony with the natural rhythms of the Earth.

Before you start, remember that your garden is a reflection of your inner self. Just like you, every garden is unique. No matter its size - whether a spacious backyard or a collection of pots on a windowsill - it holds the potential to be a sacred, magical space.

Choosing the Right Plants

To begin, carefully select the plants you wish to grow in your witch's garden. Each plant, herb, and vegetable has its own magical properties that can enhance your cooking rituals. For example, rosemary is known for its protective powers, while basil attracts wealth and happiness. Lavender helps encourage peace and calm, while thyme is linked with courage and strength.

Learn about each plant and their magical correspondences. Understand the energies they carry and how they align with your intentions. Think about what you want to manifest in your life. If you seek love, consider planting roses or strawberries. For health, consider calendula or garlic. For prosperity, consider mint or basil.

Cultivating Your Witch's Garden

Once you've selected your plants, it's time to prepare your garden. Your intention during this process is as important as the physical preparation. Begin by clearing and cleansing the area. You may wish to perform a small ritual or say a blessing to purify the space and set your intentions.

As you cultivate the soil, envision it as a fertile canvas ready to receive your seeds. Think of each stir of the earth as an infusion of your energy and intent. This is not a chore, but a sacred act of creation, a conversation between you and the Earth.

Choose a planting time that aligns with the natural rhythms of the Earth. Many witches plant by the moon phases. The new moon, a time of growth and beginnings, is often chosen for planting seeds. The full moon, a time of abundance and fruition, is ideal for harvesting.

Tending to Your Witch's Garden

Just as your magical practices require dedication and consistency, so does your witch's garden. Regular watering, pruning, and nurturing are essential. As you tend to your plants, remember that you're not just growing a garden; you're cultivating magic.

Mindfulness plays a crucial role here. When watering your plants, visualize it as a nurturing energy, encouraging growth not just in the plants, but also in your life. When you prune your plants, see it as a release of what no longer serves you, making space for new growth.

Create rituals for tending your garden. These could be as simple as greeting your plants each morning, whispering words of encouragement as they grow, or leaving offerings for the nature spirits that may dwell in your garden.

Harvesting Your Magical Bounty

When it comes to harvesting your herbs, fruits, and vegetables, timing is key. Traditionally, many witches prefer to harvest at dawn, when the world is fresh and dew-kissed, and the plants' energies are at their peak.

As you harvest, express your gratitude to the plant and to the Earth for their bounty. Remember, you're not just gathering ingredients for your next meal; you're collecting the fruits of your magical intentions, ready to be used in your kitchen witchery.

Using Your Garden's Bounty in Your Kitchen Witchery

Finally, bring your garden's bounty into your kitchen. As you use each plant in your cooking, remember its magical properties. Add basil to your sauces for prosperity, rosemary to your roasted potatoes for protection, or lavender to your desserts for peace.

As you cook, visualize your intentions manifesting, powered by the magical ingredients you've grown in your witch's garden. Feel the magic infuse into your meals, ready to nourish not just your body, but also your spirit.

Creating and cultivating your witch's garden is a rewarding journey that blends the art of gardening with the craft of the witch. As you grow your plants, you also grow in wisdom and magic, deepening your connection with nature and the energies around you. Your witch's garden becomes a sacred sanctuary, a magical powerhouse, and a source of limitless inspiration for your kitchen witchery. And remember, the most important ingredient you'll ever add to your garden is your love and intention. With these, your witch's garden will truly flourish.

Seasonal Witchery and Sabbat Feasts

In our modern world where refrigeration and international shipping have made nearly every type of produce available year-round, it's easy to lose sight of the seasonality of our food. Yet, for our ancestors, their entire diet revolved around what could be grown, harvested, or hunted in each season. This natural cycle of the earth is known as the Wheel of the Year. As a kitchen witch, reconnecting with this cycle, aligning your cooking and feasting with the seasons, and celebrating the Sabbats are powerful ways to infuse magic into your nourishment and honor the rhythms of the earth.

Understanding the Wheel of the Year

The Wheel of the Year is a representation of the earth's yearly cycle of seasons. It's comprised of eight Sabbats: four Solar Sabbats (solstices and equinoxes) and four Earth Sabbats (the midpoints between the solar festivals). Each Sabbat marks a significant point in the earth's journey around the sun and embodies distinct energies, themes, and traditional foods that are connected to that time of the year.

Imbolc

Imbolc, celebrated around February 1st, marks the beginning of spring, a time of rebirth and new beginnings. The snow begins to melt, and the first signs of spring start to appear. Traditional foods associated with Imbolc are dairy products and foods symbolizing the sun, like round-shaped baked goods, to honor the returning warmth. Think of fresh cheeses, homemade breads, and pastries. A magical meal could include a warm, home-baked bread imbued with your intentions for new beginnings, served with a selection of local cheeses.

Ostara

Celebrated around March 21st, Ostara, or the spring equinox, is a time of balance when day and night are equal. Symbolically, it's a time for growth and fertility. Foods associated with Ostara are eggs, green leafy vegetables, and sprouts. For Ostara, you could prepare a nourishing quiche filled with spring greens and fresh herbs from your garden, each ingredient charged with your intent for growth and renewal.

Beltane

Around May 1st, we celebrate Beltane, a festival of abundance and fertility. As the earth enters its most fertile period, traditional Beltane foods include honey, oats, and dairy. A beautiful Beltane feast could feature a honey-glazed roast, a creamy risotto, and a dessert of oatmeal cookies, each bite sweetened with the promise of abundance.

Litha

The summer solstice, Litha, around June 21st, is a celebration of the sun at its peak. Foods are fresh, vibrant, and full of the sun's energy. Think fresh fruits, especially berries, summer vegetables, and herbs. A Litha feast could include a colorful salad charged with intentions of joy and vitality, a main course seasoned with aromatic herbs, and a dessert of mixed berries to honor the sun's peak.

Lammas

Celebrated around August 1st, Lammas marks the beginning of the harvest season. Grain products like bread, as well as early harvested vegetables and berries, are common. For Lammas, consider baking a loaf of bread from scratch, each knead and roll charged with gratitude for the earth's abundance. Pair it with a hearty vegetable stew using the first of your harvested crops.

Mabon

Mabon, or the autumn equinox, around September 21st, is a time of balance and gratitude. Apples, root vegetables, and pumpkins are traditional foods. A Mabon meal could include a warming pumpkin soup, a root vegetable roast, and a homemade apple pie, each dish filled with your thankfulness for the year's blessings.

Samhain

Samhain, celebrated around November 1st, marks the beginning of the darker half of the year. It's a time to honor the dead and the cycle of death and rebirth. Traditional foods include apples, pumpkins, nuts, and meats. A Samhain feast might feature a hearty meat stew, roasted pumpkin, a nutty salad, and apple crumble for dessert, each bite acknowledging the cyclical nature of life and death.

Yule

The winter solstice, Yule, around December 21st, is a celebration of the return of the light as the days start to lengthen again. Traditional Yule foods are hearty, warming, and rich, like roasts, nuts, spices, and citrus fruits. A Yule feast could include a spicy citrus-glazed roast, roasted vegetables, and a rich fruitcake, each dish infused with your hopes for the coming light and new year.

When cooking for the Sabbats, it's important to remember that the purpose of these meals is not just to feed the body, but also to nourish the spirit. Each ingredient should be chosen with intention, and each step in the cooking process should be mindful and deliberate. As you stir your pot, knead your dough, or chop your vegetables, focus on the magical purpose of the meal and infuse the food with your intentions. Say a blessing over your feast before you eat, thanking the earth for its bounty and the food for its nourishment.

Celebrating the Sabbats through seasonal cooking is a beautiful way to connect with the natural world and to align your magical practice with the rhythms of the earth. As you honor each turning of the Wheel of the Year with a carefully prepared feast, you'll be weaving a powerful magic that nourishes not just your body, but also your soul. So, embrace the joy of seasonal witchery, and let your kitchen become a place of magic and transformation all year round.

Nourishing Body and Spirit: Mindful Eating

The kitchen witch's path is deeply intertwined with nourishment - both physical and spiritual. Our food is not merely sustenance, but a source of magical energy, a connection to the earth, and a way to manifest our intentions. This chapter delves into the practice of mindful eating, inviting you to explore and deepen your relationship with the food you consume.

Mindful eating, as a practice, integrates mindfulness meditation with our everyday act of eating. Instead of rushing through meals or eating while distracted, mindful eating invites us to slow down, fully engage with our food, and cultivate an awareness and appreciation of our eating experience. It is about bringing our full attention to the process of eating, from the selection of ingredients to the preparation, serving, and finally, the consumption of food.

When we eat mindfully, we make the act of eating a meditation. We focus on the aromas, the tastes, the textures, the colors, the sounds of our meals. This helps us savor every bite, every moment of our mealtime, and helps us connect with the energy our food carries.

Let's begin our journey into mindful eating with the basic principles.

Understanding and Appreciating Your Food

A mindful eater pays attention to the food on their plate. Begin by appreciating the journey your food has taken to reach you - from the seeds that were planted, to the farmers who nurtured the crops, the process of harvesting, transportation, the preparation and the cooking. Think of the energies of the earth, water, air, and fire that have been instrumental in the creation of this meal. Each element adds a different layer of energy to your food.

Take a moment to express gratitude for this journey and for all those involved in bringing this food to your table. This mindful gratitude deepens our connection to our food and to the world around us.

Being Present

As you begin your meal, center yourself in the present moment. Silence any distractions around you and within you. Remove any digital distractions, like phones or televisions, from your eating space. Close your eyes and take a deep breath, relaxing your body and calming your mind. As you open your eyes, take in the sight of your food, appreciating its colors, shapes, and textures.

Engage Your Senses

Mindful eating is a sensory experience. Start by smelling your food. The aroma of your meal is the first introduction to the flavors that await you. It's also an indicator of the quality and freshness of the ingredients used.

As you take your first bite, focus on the taste and the texture. Is it sweet, sour, bitter, or salty? Is it crunchy, soft, creamy, or chewy? Allow yourself to fully experience these sensations, instead of mindlessly chewing and swallowing.

Listen to the sounds your food makes as you eat. The crunch of a fresh vegetable or the gentle squish of ripe fruit. These sounds are part of the eating experience and being aware of them adds to our overall appreciation of the meal.

Lastly, acknowledge the aftertaste. After swallowing, what flavors linger in your mouth? Take a moment to savor this as well.

The Energy of Your Food

Remember that everything carries energy, including your food. This energy can be positive, nourishing, and healing, or it can be negative and draining. The energy in your food is influenced by several factors, including the way the food was grown and harvested, the emotions of the person who prepared it, and even the mood in which you consume it.

In kitchen witchery, we acknowledge this energy and use it in our favor. A meal prepared with love and positive intentions carries that energy and can nourish not only our bodies, but our spirits as well.

Chewing and Eating Slowly

Take your time to chew your food properly. The process of digestion begins in the mouth, and thorough chewing can aid in better digestion. Moreover, eating slowly helps us recognize our body's signals for fullness, preventing overeating.

Responding Instead of Reacting to Hunger

Mindful eating helps us differentiate between physical hunger and emotional hunger. We learn to respond to our body's cues for nourishment rather than reacting to emotional triggers for eating.

Remember, the journey to mindful eating is a gradual one. It is about shifting our relationship with food and nourishing ourselves in a holistic manner, both physically and spiritually. As kitchen witches, this mindful approach to eating helps us infuse our meals with magical intention and transform the act of eating into a nourishing ritual of love, gratitude, and mindful awareness.

Mindful eating is more than just a practice. It is a philosophy, a way of life that encourages us to respect the food we consume, our bodies that need nourishment, and the world that provides us with our sustenance. It's about recognizing and honoring the energy that our food carries, which in turn, transforms our mundane meals into magical feasts.

In the next chapter, we will explore the rituals and blessings that can help us further infuse our kitchen and our meals with positive, magical energy.

Rituals and Blessings for the Kitchen Witch

As a kitchen witch, you hold the power to turn everyday cooking and nourishment rituals into magical experiences. By invoking chants and blessings, you can infuse your kitchen and your meals with a positive, magical energy that resonates with your intentions and aspirations. This chapter will guide you through various rituals, chants, and blessings that you can adopt and adapt to your unique magical kitchen practices.

The Kitchen Blessing Ritual

Every kitchen witch's journey begins with creating a sacred space for the magical workings, and what better place to start than the heart of your home - the kitchen? This ritual is designed to cleanse your kitchen of negative energies and bless it as a haven for culinary magic.

Firstly, gather your tools - you will need a white or lavender candle (for purity and cleansing), incense or smudging herbs (such as sage or sweetgrass), and a bowl of saltwater. Begin by lighting the candle and placing it in the center of your kitchen. This will act as a beacon of positivity and light.

Next, light your incense or smudging herbs and gently waft the smoke around the room. As you do this, envision the smoke carrying away any negative energy, leaving behind a cleansed, pure space. You might want to chant, "With this sacred smoke, I cleanse this space. Negative energies, you have no place."

Then, take your bowl of saltwater (a symbol of purification) and lightly sprinkle it around the room, especially in corners or any areas that feel 'heavy'. While doing so, you could say, "With salt and water, I purify. In this kitchen, no negativity shall lie."

Finally, stand in the center of your kitchen, close your eyes, and envision a glowing white light radiating from the candle, filling the entire room. In your mind or out loud, say a blessing, "This kitchen is blessed. It is a sacred space for nourishment and magic. Let all who gather here in hunger leave with bodies and souls fulfilled."

This ritual sets a strong foundation for all the magical workings that will occur in your kitchen and can be performed regularly to maintain the positive energy.

Meal Blessing Ritual

Infusing your meals with positive intentions not only uplifts your spirits but also enhances the overall dining experience. Before eating or serving food, take a moment to bless it. Hold your hands over the meal and imagine a soft light streaming from your hands, bathing the food in its warmth. You might choose to say, "Bless this food, from earth to plate. Provide nourishment, strength, and grace."

Remember, the most important thing is that the words come from your heart and reflect your intentions.

New Utensil Blessing Ritual

When you bring a new kitchen tool into your magical workings, it's crucial to welcome it properly. Start by washing it with warm, soapy water mixed with a pinch of salt to cleanse any lingering energies. Dry it thoroughly, then hold it in your hands and close your eyes. Feel its weight, its texture, its purpose. Say a blessing like, "Blessed be this [utensil], may it serve my kitchen well. May it aid in nourishing bodies and souls, in this space where love and magic dwell."

Rituals for Cooking

Magical energy isn't just for special occasions. You can weave magic into every dish you create with a few simple practices. Whenever you stir a pot or whisk a bowl, do so in a clockwise direction to attract positivity and fulfilment. Chant your intentions, whether they're for health, happiness, love, or abundance, into your dishes as you cook.

A simple chant might be, "With this spoon, I weave the spell, into this dish, all will be well." Feel the warmth from the cooking process as a testament to the energy you're putting into your food.

As a kitchen witch, the rituals, chants, and blessings you adopt become integral parts of your culinary magic. They transform the mundane into the magical, infuse your food with intention and make your kitchen a sacred space.

Remember, kitchen witchery is a highly personal and intuitive path. These rituals are guidelines - feel free to adapt them or create your own to fit your unique practice. What matters most is your intention. As long as you pour love, gratitude, and positive energy into your cooking and nourishment, you are embracing the path of the kitchen witch.

So, roll up your sleeves, stir the pot, and let your kitchen magic come alive with these rituals and blessings. May your kitchen always be a place of nourishment, magic, and joy!

The Magic of Fermentation and Preservation

Fermentation and preservation are more than mere techniques to extend the life of food; they are rituals that capture the very essence of transformation. They invite time, patience, and understanding into your kitchen. In a sense, they serve as a metaphor for personal growth and development, both steeped in the beauty of transformation, blooming with the passage of time, and hinging on the sustenance of careful nurturing.

Fermentation, in particular, is a beautiful dance between nature and nurture. It is a process that breathes life into the simplest of ingredients, creating a complex array of flavors, textures, and health benefits. Not only does it present a cornucopia of culinary opportunities, but it also represents the magic of change and growth, the transformation from raw ingredient into a substance that is greater than the sum of its parts.

Fermentation: The Alchemical Transformation

Fermentation is a form of alchemical transformation. At its heart, it is a process of controlled decay, a dance with the natural elements where bacteria, yeasts, and fungi turn sugars into acids, gases, and alcohol. This transformation mirrors the mysteries of life, death, and rebirth—themes that resonate deeply within witchcraft.

This process is sacred and can be seen as a ritual in and of itself. When you are creating fermented foods, you are acting as a facilitator for these tiny organisms. You are setting the stage, giving them the nourishment they need, and then stepping back to let nature take its course.

In kitchen witchery, we observe and respect this process, infusing it with our intent. As we mix the salt with the cabbage to make sauerkraut, as we stir the honey and water that will become mead, we pour our intentions into the mixture. We imagine the changes that will happen, the growth, the transformation, and we align it with our personal growth and spiritual journey.

Preservation: Sealing the Magic

Preservation, in its own right, is a time capsule of magical intent. Jams, jellies, pickles, and preserves are all methods of capturing the essence of ingredients, sealing in their magic for use throughout the year.

When we preserve foods, we are capturing a moment in time, a snapshot of the season. We preserve strawberries in early summer, cucumbers in late summer, and apples in the fall. Each jar becomes a memory of that season, containing not only the flavors of the food but also the energies of that time.

In a magical context, preservation can serve as a way to store energy for later use. When we make jam from strawberries picked under the midsummer sun, we capture some of that sunlight, some of that warmth, and some of that abundant summer energy. In the depths of winter, when we open that jar, we release that energy back into our homes.

Personal Growth and Transformation

So, how do these techniques symbolize and assist in personal growth and transformation? The answer lies in understanding the processes themselves. Fermentation is not a quick process. It takes days, weeks, even months for the transformation to fully occur. The same goes for most preservation techniques.

Personal growth, like fermentation and preservation, requires time and patience. You must set your intentions, provide the right conditions, and then let the process unfold naturally. There will be periods of waiting, periods of active work, and periods of uncertainty where you wonder if you're doing it right. But with patience and faith, the transformation occurs.

By aligning our personal transformation with these processes, we tap into that same magical energy. As our sauerkraut ferments, so too do we transform. As our preserves capture the energy of the seasons, we also capture moments of our life, learning from them and growing.

When we eat these foods, we take in more than just nutrients. We take in the energy, the magic of transformation. We reinforce our commitment to personal growth and development, reminding ourselves of the journey we are on.

Fermentation and preservation are ancient techniques that are as magical as they are practical. By understanding their deeper symbolic meanings, we can incorporate them into our kitchen witch practices, infusing our food and our lives with the magic of transformation. Remember, the kitchen is more than just a place to prepare food. It is a sanctuary, a place of alchemy and magic, where everyday ingredients transform into nourishing meals, and where we, too, can transform.

Sacred Smoke: Incense and Smudging in the Kitchen

Our kitchen, as we've learned in previous chapters, is more than just a space for cooking food—it's a sacred space, a personal sanctuary where we connect with the Earth's bounty, and through careful preparation, convert it into nourishment for ourselves and loved ones. As such, it's of the utmost importance that the energy within this sacred space remains clean and clear. In this chapter, we will explore how to cleanse and consecrate your kitchen using incense and smudging, traditional practices with roots in numerous ancient cultures.

Before we begin, it's important to understand the concept of energy. Everything in the universe vibrates at a particular frequency, emanating its unique energy. The food we prepare, the tools we use, and yes, even our kitchen itself, all have a vibrational energy. Over time, negative energies can build up, resulting in a space that feels heavy, stagnant, or just plain off. It's at these times that we must cleanse and purify our spaces.

The art of cleansing with smoke, often called smudging, has been a sacred ritual in many cultures. The Native Americans used sage, cedar, and sweetgrass, while in ancient Celtic traditions, herbs like mugwort, vervain, and yarrow were preferred. In the East, resins like frankincense and myrrh have been used for thousands of years. This practice isn't just about the physical act of burning herbs or resins—it's a ritual, a sacred act of purification and dedication.

Choosing Your Smudge

Choosing what to use for your smudging ritual is a deeply personal decision. Traditional choices include sage (particularly white sage), cedar, sweetgrass, and palo santo. Each of these has its own unique properties and uses. Sage, for example, is excellent for removing negativity, while cedar is often used for protection. Sweetgrass is used to attract positive energy after a cleansing, and palo santo, a sacred wood from South America, is often used for both cleansing and attracting positive energy.

Additionally, many kitchen witches prefer to use culinary herbs in their smudging practices. Rosemary, for example, is a powerful protective and purifying herb, and its readily available nature and pleasant smell make it an excellent choice for kitchen smudging. Thyme, a potent purifier, is another excellent choice. Whatever you choose, ensure that it is sustainably sourced and, if you're using a culinary herb, not sprayed with any pesticides.

The Smudging Ritual

Before you begin, it's essential to set your intention. Are you aiming to clear out negativity, invite in positivity, or perhaps consecrate your kitchen for a particular magical working? Hold this intention firmly in your mind as you prepare your materials.

Light the end of your smudge stick, or if you're using loose herbs, place them on a heat-proof dish and light them, ensuring you have a good amount of smoke. Start at the door of your kitchen and slowly walk around the space, allowing the smoke to waft into each corner. As you do so, visualize the smoke clearing away all the negative energy, sweeping it out of the windows and doors, leaving only clean, bright energy behind.

As you move around your kitchen, you can say a simple chant or incantation, such as:

"By the purifying power of this sacred smoke,

May all negativity be gone in a stroke.

By the power of air, fire, water, and earth,

I cleanse this space for all it's worth."

Remember to smudge your cooking tools as well, holding each in the smoke for a few moments while visualizing any negative energy being drawn out and replaced with vibrant, positive energy.

Once you've cleansed your entire kitchen, take a moment to ground and center yourself. Feel the clean, bright energy of your newly purified kitchen, and hold gratitude in your heart for the sacred act you've just performed.

Incense in the Kitchen

In addition to smudging, incense is another tool that can be used to cleanse and consecrate your kitchen space. Traditional incenses like frankincense, myrrh, or sandalwood can be used, as well as any incense that aligns with your current intention.

Like smudging, using incense is more than just lighting it and letting it burn. It's a ritual, a sacred act. As you light your incense, hold your intention firmly in your mind. Visualize the smoke from the incense carrying your intention up to the universe, where it is heard and acknowledged.

As the incense burns, walk around your kitchen, allowing the smoke to permeate every corner. As you do so, say a simple chant or incantation, such as:

"By the power of this sacred incense,

I cleanse this space, its energy intense.

Purify, consecrate, make it pure and bright,

May this kitchen shine with magical light."

Using incense in this way not only cleanses your kitchen but also adds a layer of intention and purpose to your cooking. It's a way of inviting the divine, the magic, into your everyday routine, infusing every meal you prepare with a touch of the sacred.

Remember, the act of smudging or burning incense is a sacred ritual. Treat it with respect and reverence. These acts are not about "getting rid of the bad," but rather about creating a space that vibrates at its highest potential—a space that invites in the energies that serve you, your intentions, and your magical workings. As you perform these rituals, hold space for the transformation and watch as your kitchen, the heart of your home, becomes a glowing beacon of your personal magic.

The Kitchen Witch's Book of Shadows

In your journey as a kitchen witch, you have learned to see the kitchen as not just a place for cooking and nourishing your body but also a sanctuary where you nourish your soul. You have experienced the magic of the culinary world, and you understand that each ingredient, each meal, is a sacred act of magic in itself. It's time to document your magical culinary journey. That's where the Kitchen Witch's Book of Shadows comes into play.

The Book of Shadows, or Grimoire, is a sacred tool in witchcraft. It's a personal journal where witches document their spells, rituals, correspondences, and experiences. The book holds a record of their magical journey, and it becomes a testament to their growth, knowledge, and wisdom. As a kitchen witch, your Book of Shadows will be a little different. Along with magical rituals and spells, it will contain your recipes, your experiences with different ingredients, the intuitive insights you gained while cooking, and the transformation you witnessed within yourself and others through your culinary creations.

Creating Your Kitchen Witch's Book of Shadows

Creating your Kitchen Witch's Book of Shadows is a personal and intimate act. Choose a book that resonates with you. It could be a beautifully bound journal, an old recipe book with space for notes, or a digital journal if you prefer typing over writing. You could decorate your book to reflect your personality, using drawings, stickers, or pressed herbs and flowers. The aim is to make your book feel like it's a part of you.

Documenting Your Recipes

Your book of shadows will serve as a repository for all your magical recipes. Write down each recipe you have tried, including the list of ingredients, their magical properties, and the intention behind the meal. Document the process of cooking, and any specific instructions to infuse magic into your dishes. Did you stir your soup clockwise to attract positive energy? Did you bake your bread during a specific moon phase? These are details worth noting down.

Capturing Your Experiences

Cooking is a sensory experience that engages sight, smell, taste, touch, and hearing. When you're writing about a particular dish, recount the sensory details. How did the dough feel beneath your fingertips? What was the aroma that filled your kitchen when you roasted the spices? Such details will bring your experiences alive when you revisit your entries in the future.

Insights and Intuitive Messages

As you cook intuitively, you may receive insights or messages. It could be a sudden understanding of a problem you were facing, or a deep knowing of something you need to do. These intuitive messages are valuable, and it's essential to jot them down immediately. Over time, you'll begin to see patterns in these messages, helping you understand your intuition better.

Rituals, Spells, and Magic

Your kitchen witch's Book of Shadows should also include your kitchen-based rituals and spells. Whether it's a simple morning ritual of blessing your tea or an elaborate spell to banish negative energy from your kitchen, it all finds a place in your book. Write down the steps of your rituals, the tools you used, the incantations you spoke, and the results you observed.

Correspondences and Moon Phases

Just like traditional witchcraft, kitchen witchery also relies on correspondences. It could be the correspondence between different herbs and magical intentions, or between different moon phases and types of meals. Create a section in your book to jot down these correspondences for easy reference.

Your Book of Shadows as a Guide

The Kitchen Witch's Book of Shadows is a testament to your growth as a witch and as a cook. It charts your journey from maybe not knowing how to boil an egg to being able to whip up a feast that not only nourishes the body but also the soul.

Your book is also your guide. On days when you feel lost or unsure, it offers comfort and guidance. It reminds you of your past achievements and challenges you overcame. It helps you understand how far you've come and guides you on where to go next.

Keeping Your Book of Shadows

Treat your book with respect and keep it in a safe place. Some witches prefer to keep their books a secret, only sharing it with trusted fellow witches. Others may choose to pass their knowledge on to the next generation, treating the book as a family heirloom.

Remember, there is no right or wrong way to keep your book. The key is to make it as personal and representative of you as possible. As long as it serves its purpose of being a guide and record of your magical culinary journey, you're on the right track.

A Kitchen Witch's Book of Shadows is a reflection of your relationship with food and magic. Every page tells a story, not just of the meals you have prepared but of the love, magic, and intention you poured into them. It's a sacred book that holds the essence of your journey as a kitchen witch. It's your magical legacy, something that, over the years, will become an inseparable part of your witchcraft and your life. Happy writing!

Kitchen Witch Meditations

Kitchen witchery, at its heart, is about infusing our daily routines with magic and mindfulness. In the busy hum of the modern world, the act of cooking can become an oasis of calm, a sanctuary where we reconnect with ourselves, our food, and the energies of the universe. Meditation, with its emphasis on mindfulness, aligns beautifully with the spirit of the kitchen witch. This chapter will explore various meditation techniques tailored to foster mindfulness, gratitude, and a deep connection with the energy of food.

Let's begin with a foundational principle. Mindful Presence

In the heart of kitchen witchery is an awareness of the present. Mindfulness is a meditation technique that allows us to remain present and absorb the experience entirely. When cooking, take a moment to pause and observe. Take in the colors of the vegetables, the aroma of the herbs, the texture of the bread dough under your hands. Each sensation is a gateway to the present moment.

One way to foster mindful presence is the Five Senses Meditation.

Begin by finding a comfortable position in your kitchen. It might be on a chair, a stool, or even the floor - wherever you can sit comfortably and peacefully. Close your eyes and take a few deep breaths, allowing the sounds of the kitchen to fill your awareness.

What do you hear? Is it the ticking of a kitchen clock? The bubbling of a boiling pot? Each sound anchors you in the present.

Next, bring your attention to smell. Perhaps you perceive the aroma of coffee, or the subtle scent of fresh produce. Each breath in explores these scents more deeply.

Now, open your eyes and look around you. Notice the colors and shapes. Take in the detail of the grain on a wooden spoon or the vibrant hue of freshly picked tomatoes.

Then, reach out and touch. Feel the coolness of a metal bowl, the warmth of a freshly baked loaf, or the rough texture of salt crystals.

Lastly, if you have some food ready, taste it. Take a small bite and let it rest on your tongue. Experience the flavors in detail - the sweetness, sourness, bitterness, saltiness, or umami.

By engaging each of our senses, we ground ourselves in the present, turning cooking from a routine task into a rich, meditative experience.

Next, let's explore Gratitude Meditation.

We often take for granted the food that ends up on our plates. Gratitude meditation allows us to acknowledge and appreciate the journey our food has taken to nourish us.

Begin by closing your eyes and taking a few deep breaths. Hold a piece of food in your hands, perhaps an apple or a handful of grains. Visualize its journey. Imagine the seed in the soil, the sun and rain that helped it grow, the hands that harvested it. Feel the weight of the food in your hands and acknowledge its purpose to nourish and sustain you. Say a word of thanks to each element of this journey - the earth, the weather, the farmers, and even the grocers who brought it to you.

Gratitude, expressed through meditation, magnifies the magic inherent in your cooking, aligning your energy with the universal flow.

Lastly, let's delve into Energy Infusion Meditation.

Every ingredient carries an inherent energy or magical property. A kitchen witch not only understands these properties but knows how to harness them in her cooking.

Before you start cooking, hold each ingredient in your hand and close your eyes. Feel its energy. Is it vibrant and dynamic like chili? Or is it calm and comforting like chamomile? Visualize this energy as a glowing light moving from the ingredient to your hand, infusing you with its qualities. As you mix and stir, imagine this energy spreading throughout the dish.

This meditation helps you become more in tune with the energy of your food, transforming your meals into magical infusions that embody your intentions.

Through mindful presence, gratitude, and energy infusion meditations, kitchen witchery becomes more than just a way of cooking. It turns into a powerful spiritual practice, bringing you closer to your inner self, your environment, and the cosmos. Remember, every meal is a spell, every sip a potion. As a kitchen witch, you are not just feeding the body, but also nourishing the spirit. Let your kitchen become your sanctuary, and every meal a magical ritual.

Just as the cauldron bubbles and transforms ingredients into something new, let these meditations transform your everyday cooking into a deeply nourishing, magical experience. Remember to remain patient with yourself on this journey, as each meditation will deepen and enrich your connection with the food, yourself, and the world around you over time.

The kitchen is a sacred space where we make magic every day, infusing love, care, and intention into the food we prepare.

Let these meditations serve as your guide to creating a deeper connection with the divine, the magic that exists within and around you, and most importantly, the magic in your kitchen.

Embracing the Path of the Kitchen Witch

As we approach the conclusion of our journey through the intricacies of kitchen witchery, we find ourselves standing at a moment of self-reflection. It is time to take a step back and look at the path that lies before us, an enchanted path where magic is woven into the very essence of everyday nourishment.

Embracing the path of the Kitchen Witch is not simply about mastering recipes or memorizing the metaphysical properties of herbs and spices.

Rather, it is about recognizing the intrinsic magic present within ourselves and in the world around us. The kitchen, our sacred space, is not a separate realm where we only occasionally practice our craft; it is a mirror reflecting the harmony between our inner selves and the universal energies.

At the heart of kitchen witchery lies the simple, yet profound act of creation. The kitchen witch realizes that every meal prepared, every cup of tea brewed, and every loaf of bread baked is an opportunity to manifest their will into the world. It is through this creative process that you have the power to nourish not just the body, but the spirit as well.

The act of cooking is transformed into a sacred ritual, each step filled with intention. As you stir your pot, know that you are not just blending ingredients; you are weaving together energies, creating a magical concoction infused with your intentions. When you chop your vegetables, visualize releasing and harnessing their elemental energies. As you spice your dishes, imagine the magical attributes of the spices igniting, adding layers of intention into your culinary creations.

This is the dance of the kitchen witch, where mundane actions become deeply magical.

When we speak of embracing the path, we refer to the acceptance of this unique blend of the magical and the mundane. It is an acknowledgment that magic is not confined to grand rituals or elaborate spells but can be found in the simple acts of everyday life.

As you continue your journey as a kitchen witch, remember to find joy in the process. Embrace the dance of creation and destruction, of blending and separating, of heating and cooling. Delight in the scent of herbs and spices, the sizzle of a pan, the taste of a well-cooked meal. For it is through joy that our magical work is amplified. It is through joy that we raise energy, not just within our dishes, but within ourselves as well.

Each dish you create is not just a meal; it is a physical manifestation of your intentions, your wishes, and your magic. As you sit down to eat, take a moment to acknowledge the journey of your food, from the earth to your plate, and the magic that has been woven into each bite. As you nourish your body, visualize the magic within your meal nourishing your spirit, fueling your intentions and manifestations.

Along your path, there will be moments of doubt, where the way forward might seem unclear, where your magic feels lost. In these moments, return to your kitchen. Return to the simple act of cooking, of nourishing, and you will find your magic waiting for you. For in the heart of the kitchen witch, magic is never truly lost; it is simply waiting to be found again.

As we conclude this book, remember, your journey does not end here. In fact, you are just at the beginning of your magical culinary exploration. Beyond these pages, there are countless herbs to discover, recipes to try, and magical meals to create. The world of the kitchen witch is a vast one, filled with unlimited possibilities. So, continue to learn, continue to create, continue to weave your magic into every bite.

And finally, share your magic. Share your creations with others, for food is a universal language that transcends barriers. When you share your magical meals, you are not just sharing food; you are sharing a part of your spirit, a part of your magic. And in doing so, you are weaving threads of connection, threads of community.

Embrace the path of the kitchen witch with open arms, with an open heart. Discover the magic that lies in the everyday act of cooking, find joy in the process, and remember, the most magical ingredient you can add to any dish is love. So, go forth, and infuse magic into your nourishment, one dish at a time. For in the world of the kitchen witch, every meal is a spell, every bite, a magical journey.

Printed in Great Britain
by Amazon

34709301R00057